UNIVERSITY MENTAL HEALTH AND MINDSET

CONNOR WHITELEY

No part of this book may be reproduced in any form or by any electronic or mechanical means. Including information storage, and retrieval systems, without written permission from the author except for the use of brief quotations in a book review.

This book is NOT legal, professional, medical, financial or any type of official advice.

Any questions about the book, rights licensing, or to contact the author, please email connorwhiteley@connorwhiteley.net

Copyright © 2023 CONNOR WHITELEY

All rights reserved.

DEDICATION
Thank you to all my readers without you I couldn't do what I love.

INTRODUCTION

Whenever people think of university, the first thing to come to mind is the clubbing, drinking and learning that happens at university. And that definitely happens, but there is another area of university that is extremely important but it ever so rarely gets mentioned.

Since at university, it can be a very stressful time in a person's life and this can damage a person's mental health. But thankfully with the right support you can get through this with relative ease if you know who to turn to.

In addition, how to improve or the mindset needed to be a successful student at university is never mentioned as well.

So the entire point of this book in my *Psychology Student's Guide To University Series*, is exactly what the title says and this book is definitely aimed most at psychology students.

Since as we all study psychology we live in the

world and discipline of and study human behaviour and that includes mindset and other mental processes.

Therefore, the focus of this book is for you to understand how to look after your mental health at university, who to turn to if you need it and what's the mindset of a successful student. And I'm personally very glad that mindsets and attitudes can be taught. That's what the second half of this book covers.

Why Bother Reading This Book?

That's definitely a great question but I can assure you as a current psychology student at university. I have tried to find resources on mental health, mindset and how to improve as a university student, and I have had very little luck.

Since most university resources are written by academics and aren't designed to be very student friendly, as well as they always lack the student perspective. And none of them are conversational or personal.

Even though this book is mainly filled with blog posts I wrote for the brilliant online e-learning platform Active Class, I have added an introduction to each post that explains why that chapter specifically applies to psychology students.

As well as each chapter is written in a great, easy-to-understand and most importantly conversational and engaging way.

This couldn't be further away from the dull boring textbooks we all know and love as psychology students.

This book is a lot more engaging and interesting!

Who Is This Book For?

Now whilst this book is definitely aimed and written for psychology students. Everyone who is thinking of going to university in the future or are currently studying at university can get something out of this book.

Due to this is the thing about mental health. No one is immune to it and everyone can suffer from time to time, so it's always important to look after yourself.

And the information in this book can definitely help.

Of course, this book is never any sort of professional advice. But it's all still extremely useful and it signposts you to official and recommended services.

Who Wrote This Book?

Personally, I always prefer to know who wrote the nonfiction book I'm currently reading so I know the information comes from a good source.

I'm Connor Whiteley, an author of over 30 psychology books and the host of The Psychology World Podcast where each week we examine a fascinating psychology topic. As well as the podcast can be found on all major podcast apps and YouTube.

However, most importantly in this case, I am a psychology student studying at the University of

Kent, England for a number of years now. So I definitely know what the university life, highs and lows are like!

So now we all know each other, let's get started and learn about mental health and mindset at university!

PART ONE: MENTAL HEALTH

HOW TO MAINTAIN MENTAL HEALTH FOR UNIVERSITY STUDENTS?

For the first chapter of this book, I wanted to draw on a post that really does introduce and highlight some of the things we're going to be talking about in later chapters. Like imposter syndrome and the importance of socialisation.

And as psychology students, it's always important for us to understand mental health because this is what a lot of you might be interested in.

So as you're reading this blog post bear in mind that your own mental health is very important and there are lots of other great topics we'll cover later on.

Enjoy!

<u>How To Maintain Mental Health For University Students:</u>

As I write this in mid-May 2022, it is mental health awareness month and because I normally write so much about mental health on my podcast and in my books. It can be very difficult to remember what I have and have not mentioned for this blog, so I wanted to create a post where all the information was in one place. If you're a university student wanting to protect and maintain your mental health then this is a great post for you.

Note: as always this blog is not professional or any sort of official advice, and if you are struggling with your mental health then please seek professional help.

Why Is Mental Health Important For University Students?

To put it simply when students come to university and are studying throughout their degree, they will be placed in a very different environment. For example, you might have moved away from home for the first time, you might not have any friends at your new university, you might struggle to keep up with what your degree demands and so on. Including you might be struggling with imposter syndrome.

All these factors might be liberating and interesting for some. Personally moving away from home was not a big deal for me because I've always been highly independent, but it was still great to go home and see the family throughout the year.

However, some people these might be factors that you struggle with. For instance, moving away from home for the first time can be a very scary thing to do, and you might feel lonely.

That's why mental health is important to look at

so whatever you face you can be somewhat prepared on how to deal with it.

But most mental health-related topics like the ones in this post, focus on a different angle.

They focus on preventative measures.

How To Protect Your Mental Health?

Whilst different facets of the next few sections would have been mentioned in other posts, this will focus on these topics from the mental health viewpoint. As well as the last section is a must-read, it's very interesting.

Work-Life Balance

This almost goes without saying these days but considering May is not only Mental Health Awareness Month, but the start of the exam season. This is even more important, because you need to remember to study, revise but socialise too.

As a result, if you don't socialise or take a break. You will burn out, hate your studying and you will harm yourself for the long term. As well as you will hardly do your mental health any favours but creating all this psychological distress for yourself.

Therefore, please remember to study but make sure you have breaks too. Make sure you go out with friends, watch a film or just do something else that is not university-related.

There is a bit more information in How To Be Kind To Yourself During Exam Season.

However, when it comes to mental health, making sure you prevent a meltdown, unneeded stress and more. You do need to take your work-life balance seriously, and please know that doing all-nighters does not make you a good student. Sure it might make you feel like one, but it won't do you any good.

Just bear that in mind.

<u>Socialising and Combating Loneliness</u>

I'm pretty sure there is a loneliness blog post coming in the next few weeks but university can be a very lonely time for people. Especially people who don't want to go out to clubs, bars and do the whole drinking side of university.

As well as making friends can be difficult for people to as there isn't a very set way of meeting people and actually engaging with them. Due to we're all university students here and we can all remember times when we all just went to the lecture theatre, barely anyone spoke to each other and then we all left.

For people who struggle to make friends as it is, that is hardly helpful.

Resulting in an increased risk of loneliness and all the mental health difficulties that that creates for people.

Thankfully, because of how universities are set up (at least UK universities), there is a wide-ranging set of ways to help fix this problem. The most obvious being that people should try to engage and talk more with their fellow students on their courses. I know that is hard but you'll be surprised by where some conversations can lead you.

Also it's a good thing that UK universities have societies (social clubs) formed around a particular activity so you can almost always find like-minded people who are into the same things as you. I've met plenty of great people throughout societies.

The only slightly negative thing I will say is you do need to be aware that some universities do not update their society listing to get rid of the ones that are closed. I was a little disappointed when I first started my university because there were plenty of amazing sounding societies, but they were closed.

Equally, there are some great ones that are open, filled with great people and you definitely fill less lonely after going to a society event.

Reading

With my podcast being psychology focused, mental health does pop up rather often (because it's what me and my listeners enjoy) so I wanted to share two posts with you from the early days of the podcast.

As a result of whilst I'm surprised I haven't covered stress since 2020 (a very stressful year indeed!) there was one episode that discussed a brand new study at the time that found the most effective stress relief was *reading*.

Then you might find New Ways To Deal With Stress useful too.

As a frequent reader (who always has a scarily big reading pile) I can testify to the powerful relaxing nature of reading. Because the problem with modern

English teaching in school is it kills a lot of people's enjoyment for reading, because people think they have to analyse everything they read.

No!

And there is nothing better than enjoying a great book by some great authors. A book that can transport you to another gripping world with loveable characters and endings that are just perfect, and leave you wanting more.

As we're on the topic of mental health, reading makes perfect sense why it would be relaxing and protect mental health. Due to the entire point of commercial and genre fiction is to be escapist, and given how your real life can be what is causing you the stress. Reading is the perfect way to escape your real life and relax for a few hours.

Therefore, I cannot recommend reading enough to help mental health. And with it being the summer soon, if your friends and family are busy (and you have a garden), then read in the garden for a bit. That's very relaxing.

Finally, if you want some book recommendations, please check out:

Facebook for weekly recommendations from top authors

Instagram for weekly recommendations

My own range of science fiction, fantasy, mystery and sweet romance books.

Conclusion:

As mentioned before, mental health is something to take seriously, but you can really improve it if you simply take a few steps and adopt them into your lifestyle. Make sure you maintain a good work-life balance, you socialise and combat loneliness and it never hurts to read.

If you start adopting some of these tips now, you might be able to avoid a lot of distress down the road.

And isn't that what we want?

HOW TO FIND MENTAL HEALTH SUPPORT SERVICES AT UNIVERSITY?

This is one of those chapters where I know a lot of people will not be interested in learning about mental health services. Yet as psychology students I am a bit more hopeful that you will all read it and at least acknowledge that these are important to know.

These might not be important at first to know but I would feel a lot better if people at least where aware of the mental health support options available to you. Just in case you undergo a mental health crisis.

Because no matter how "hard", manly (perhaps) or whatever society teaches us about mental health that makes both men and women unlikely to come forward, I want you to know that your mental health matters.

And sometimes even the strongest of people need a little help, and it sure as hell doesn't make you weak.

How To Find Mental Health Support Services For University Students?

It is a sad truth that because of university deadlines, personal reasons, university workload amongst other reasons. This can cause university students to experience mental health difficulties and they can suffer. Whilst the support services differ between different universities and different countries, I'm going to talk about some general support services before mentioning some country-specific ones towards the end.

But before all that, as a clinical psychology student, I have to stress it is perfectly okay to experience mental health difficulties. It doesn't make you messed up, a failure or any of the other negative terms used to describe mental health sufferers.

(Personally, I think it shows courage to ask for help with your mental health because it's a difficult thing to do!)

Your University:

At least in the United Kingdom, and I have little doubt it would be different in other countries, but all universities that I know of have a support service. At my university, it's called Student Support and Wellbeing, and this is a great place to go if you're struggling because these people will help you.

Therefore, you might want to check out your own university to see if there's a similar support service that allows you to go and talk to someone. Then they might be able to give you some ideas about what to do next.

A Student Helpline

This is another fairly common one where students volunteer to answer calls on a helpline that you can call. Meaning you get to talk to other students about your difficulties and they can provide some advice to you.

I think this has a number of unique benefits because to some extent you might find it easier to talk to someone over the phone compared to in person. As well as it's like there's an extra layer of anonymity and confidentiality about using a helpline because the person you're talking to never sees your face. This might make you more comfortable.

In addition, you might find it easier to talk to another student about your difficulties because you have shared experiences and they can relate to you more.

National Mental Health Services

This is where this blog post diverts from globally applicable information and focuses more on the United Kingdom and the United States (sorry everyone else). For the sole purpose of it's easier to find information for these countries.

Therefore, I'm very thankful that for the most part these two countries do value mental health and each one has a national mental health service that you can call if you need it. Then you'll get to talk to a trained member of staff or volunteer about your difficulties and they can help you.

For example, if you're a university student in the UK then you might want to call:

Mind.org.uk
Samaritans

Then for students in the United States, I'm sure there are lots of state mental health services and it differs from state to state. But I managed to find these two national ones that could be useful.

Mental Health Foundation
Mental Health American

Conclusion:

Whilst this was a short blog post, I really hope it gave you some ideas about how to find mental health support services so you can look after yourself if you need it. Because your mental health is as important as your physical health and it cannot be ignored.

Additionally, as an ending note, nothing in this blog post was any sort of official advice and this blog isn't affiliated with any of the mentioned mental health organisations.

I hope you found it useful.

Have a great day!

HOW TO PREVENT LONELINESS AT UNIVERSITY?

Whether you're a brand new psychology student or a student that has been studying psychology for a few years, we are all aware that loneliness is a killer, it can have horrific consequences for mental health and more.

Therefore, please don't skip this next chapter because it is absolutely critical.

<u>How To Prevent Loneliness At University?</u>

Whilst university can definitely be the best time in a student's life because of the freedom, growth and learning opportunities that it gives you. University can be a very lonely time for university students too, and that's the focus for this blog post so (hopefully) you'll never have to experience this.

<u>Why Can University Be Lonely?</u>

This is something that lots of people don't understand, be it family members, students who are naturally popular and make friends with ease (lucky them) and people who are going to university with people they already know.

However, university can be a lonely place for students for a range of reasons. Like, they're moving to a brand new area with no one they know, they're having problems "clicking" with people and they just haven't found where they fit in yet.

Therefore, the rest of the post will focus on how do we deal with and avoid some of these issues.

How To Prevent Loneliness At University?
Go To The Socials And Other University Events:

I must admit I am terrible for this point but I have been to a couple, and I can honestly say they are great. You get to meet tons of new people who do the same subject as you, and you can get into some very good conversations. Be it about the subject itself, your favourite parts, areas you hate (that can be a great icebreaker).

Then once you've broken that ice, you can easily talk to them about other things. For example, I went to one earlier in the academic year and naturally I started talking about psychology as a whole. But after ten minutes, I was talking to this woman about politics, beliefs and lots of other things.

Therefore, I know (believe me) that these university socials can seem… intimidating, especially as a non-drinker. Since all throughout society, the constant thing we hear about university is all the partying, drinking and other things that I'm (as a non-drinker) aren't interested. But I really do encourage you to go because they can be great fun, interesting and definitely worth your time.

I'll definitely be going to more in the future. And I recommend you go to some to, at least give it a try.

<u>Join Societies</u>

This is definitely a UK-centric point but I can't see why there wouldn't be other things in other countries. As well as the easiest way to think about societies are social clubs formed around an activity. Be it drinking, cooking, sports or something else entirely.

Now these are brilliant for social opportunities and meeting new people, because you get to meet people doing different courses. And this allows you to learn about how their degrees work, what their subject is like and you can learn plenty of interesting things like that, even before you start getting people to talk about themselves.

Also one of my favourite things was you get to meet people from different cultures even more in different societies.

Additionally, if you're from an ethnic minority or LGBT+ group and are concerned about not being able to find people like you. There are normally a fair amount of groups for you at university, so that is definitely a good place to meet others.

Therefore, I really recommend you do check out what your university offers and go to some events. These are great ways to meet people, get you out and help you feel a little less lonely.

Get A Part-Time Job

There is (or will be) a blog post on *How To Get A Part-Time Job* at some point, but I do recommend this option for everyone. Not only would you be earning yourself some money, which is really great, but it gives you a chance to experience new things with new people.

For example, I've met lots of great people through my work as a Student Ambassador for the university. I've met people who I never would have met otherwise and they've all been great.

If you focus on loneliness for a second, then part-time jobs can be really helpful in getting you out, mixing with people and because you'll be spending so much time with them. You might make a friend or two, or at least learn that you aren't the only person feeling like this.

Since (on a side note) the sad truth about loneliness at university is when we all have our *Welcome To University Talks* as I like to call them. Yes, we hear so much about loneliness, what to do about it, etc. But until you actually experience it even a little, and do something about it. Then no one can know what it is or even think about how to deal with it.

Overall, getting a part-time job can be useful because it makes you go to work, mix and work with new people. As well as it has the great benefit of earning you some money too!

And come on, who doesn't like extra money?

Push Yourself And Conclusion

To wrap up this post, I just want to stress the importance of pushing yourself out of your comfort zone. I know that going to a brand new place with no one you know is a bit concerning and sometimes it can feel better to just stay and mix with your flatmates. But I do strongly, strongly encourage you to go out of your way to meet new people, because it will be worth it in the long run.

You never know what people you'll meet, the impact they'll have on your life and what friends you could make unless you go out of your comfort zone, and make a strong effort to meet new people.

HOW TO OVERCOME IMPOSTER SYNDROME

If you were like me when I first started university, you never ever thought it was possible for *you* to have imposter syndrome. But I can assure you at some point you will suffer from imposter syndrome and it can be awful.

That's why this next chapter focuses on how to overcome Imposter Sydrome so you hopefully can quickly bounce back from what can potentially destroy a lot of university students' career before they even begin.

How to Overcome Imposter Syndrome For University Students?

Imposter Syndrome will almost always happen at university and when it does strike it can be very damaging and lead to a decrease in mental health. No one wants this to happen, so in this blog post, you're going to learn what Imposter Syndrome is and most importantly, how to overcome it!

What Is Imposter Syndrome?

Imposter Syndrome is when a person doesn't feel like they belong where they are and they underappreciate their achievements to the point where they feel like imposters at the workplace or university. As well as people believe they aren't as competent or intelligent as other people at university.

I hate to admit this but this is extremely common at university and it always strikes at some point. Because during my first week or two at university, I had a lecture on this topic as the lecturers wanted to kill off any imposter syndrome, and at the time I didn't have any imposter syndrome.

However, towards the end of my first term, I remember suffering from it badly one night and my mental health was gone.

Hopefully, by the end of the blog post, you won't have to go through that.

Why Is Imposter Syndrome Important?

The main reason why Imposter Syndrome must be addressed is because it can lead to decreases in mental health, which is never good. For example, people with Imposter Syndrome can suffer from mental health conditions. Like, depression and anxiety.

Yet another reason is because Imposter Syndrome can lead to the person not achieving their potential and growing. Since the fear caused by the Imposter Syndrome holds them back and it can stop them from pursuing opportunities that would allow them to grow in relationships, work and other areas of life.

How To Overcome Imposter Syndrome?

I suppose I was fortunate enough with my Imposter Syndrome that it passed overnight but I know lots of people aren't that lucky. Additionally, I have the mindset that I know I'll never be the best but as long as I keep learning, trying and doing my best then that's okay. And this is the key when it comes to overcoming Imposter Syndrome.

As a result of Imposter Syndrome is a mindset so addressing your beliefs about your abilities and perceptions is critical. As well as you need to stop comparing yourself to other people because Imposter Syndrome mainly comes from doubting your own abilities and not seeing yourself as, as good as other people.

Therefore, one of the most important things to remember is no one is perfect so please stop comparing yourself to others. Try your best on everything you do but acknowledge you will never be perfect and someone will always know more than you in some areas, and you will know more in other areas.

That's okay. It's okay not to know it all and be perfect. That's part of being human, and most of all, it's what makes learning fun. Because you will never stop learning.

<u>Conclusion:</u>

Whilst this has been a short blog post on Imposter Syndrome, I hope this has given you what you needed to fight off Imposter Syndrome or start to. There are lots of resources on the internet and Psychology Today on Imposter Syndrome.

But my unofficial advice would be just to acknowledge you're an amazing person that deserves to be where you are today, and you will never be perfect. Yet that's okay. No one is perfect so please stop putting yourself down for these unreasonably high expectations.

HOW TO KEEP YOURSELF HAPPY DURING LEARNING AT UNIVERSITY?

Whilst I don't actually have a problem with the introduction for this post, I do want to mention how this relates to psychology students. Since at some point in your university life you will have a piece of coursework. Be it a social psychology essay, a biological psychology poster or a statistical report to write up, and you will very quickly realise how not happy that makes you.

Now I mentioned not happy because it might not make you sad. But if you don't necessarily feel happy at university then this can negatively impact your grades, so that's why this next chapter is rather important to read.

Enjoy!

<u>Keeping Yourself Happy Whilst Learning For University Students</u>

Whilst I fully admit this is a strange blog post idea, because no one ever thinks about their happiness when they're learning, when I started to think more and more about the topic, I realised this was a small but very powerful topic that could make an important difference to your learning and, by extension, grades.

We all know that being happy is important because when we're happy (or at least contempt) our engagement is high, we're motivated to focus on what we're doing and generally speaking we concentrate and learn more. Making it important to look at happiness when we talk about learning, as without happiness our learning suffers.

Note: however, I must encourage you to read or listen [to this article](#) on my website because it talks about myths around happiness and why you shouldn't be sad about not being happy. For the purposes of this blog post, happiness can be interchanged with contempt and any positive emotion that will enhance your learning.

How Can You Keep Yourself Happy Whilst Learning?

Keep It Visually Interesting

Whilst this isn't a tip that works for me, I know it works for a lot of people so I need to mention it. A lot of people like to use coloured pens, highlighters and more colourful things to keep their learning interesting for them, and the colours make them happy.

This is a great tip because it means it keeps people engaged, interested and they want to be learning so they can continue to use the colours.

That's critical!

In learning you should want to continue with your learning because you want to. We've all been in situations when we want to continue but because the topic is boring, we don't. So using colours and keeping it interesting is a great workaround.

Overall, when it comes to keeping up happiness, and by extension engagement, focus and concentration, keeping it visually interesting is a great tip.

<u>Be Tidy and Smart (Environmental Factors)</u>

These environmental factors, like the tidiness of your desk, how you're dressed and more, really do impact your learning and I'm surprised how students with messy desks can learn effectively.

Because in my experience, I learn best when I have a clean desk that isn't full of distractions, well-lit (otherwise I find the darkness drains my interest) and I'm not struggling to move because my desk or work area is packed full of rubbish.

All in all, I want you to understand that when you want to learn make sure you aren't in a place that's full of distractions and isn't optimised for your learning.

At the end of the day, only you know what works for you. But for me I don't like to study or learn in a dark, distraction-filled space because I'm not happy in that situation and my engagement, focus and concentration decreases to the point that I don't learn anymore.

Pressure and Active Class

Another factor we can all relate to is pressure and this always sucks the joy out of learning or it makes us unhappy. I'm talking about the times when we have lots of things to do, like 5 chapters to read, two essays and 3 seminars to prepare for. (I'm glad I've never been in that position before)

This pressure means we get concerned about the fact we have so much to do, we don't know if we can get it all done and we get sad about it!

We don't enjoy having all of this pressure.

Thankfully, this is extremely rare to have that much pressure but you get the general idea, having other things on our mind can make us not happy during learning.

This is where Active Class is useful because it allows you to prioritise your workload, schedule things and it means you can clearly see what you need to do so you plan effectively.

In other words, Active Class allows you to avoid all of these problems so you can focus on your learning.

Conclusion:

Even after writing this post I still admit this isn't an area that's often thought about during learning. We always focus on concentration, distractions, focus and more, but we never look at how we feel when we learn. That's important to think about because if you aren't happy or contempt during learning then the other factors like engagement, focus and concentration will fail.

Therefore, at the end of this blog post, I want to stress that you should keep your learning visually interesting, focus on your learning environment and use Active Class as this should all benefit your learning in the long term.

And perhaps the most important reason to be happy whilst learning is, life's too short to be sad when learning, so find a way to have fun and be happy!

THE IMPORTANCE OF FEELING GOOD AND SELF-SATISFACTION IN LEARNING

This is definitely one of those chapters where you might not see the point in it at first and especially by the title.

However, as the introduction is very good for explaining why this chapter is so important. All I want to say is for psychology students specifically, a psychology degree is extremely rewarding and you learn such amazing things.

But realising that requires an attitude that this chapter most certainly helps out with.

The Importance Of Feeling Good And Self-Satisfaction In Learning

You might want to save this blog post for the inevitable days when you feel down and sad at university, because I'm sorry to say that will happen at some point. But feeling good and being satisfied in learning is critical for your university success.

I've already done lots of Mindset posts (starting

with What Is The University Mindset?), but this focuses more on feeling good and being satisfied with yourself.

Why Is This Important?

It all comes down to engagement and motivation. Since if you feel sad and like you're wasting your time then you don't be engaged in your studies and you won't have the motivation to learn. Leading to you learning less, not bothering with university and your grades will almost certainly fall.

I don't want that for you. You don't want that for yourself.

This is why we need to talk about how to feel good and being self-satisfied with your learning.

Reasons and Solutions For Why You're Not Feeling Good Or Self-Satisfied With Your Learning?

I remember when I was feeling down about learning and university as a whole, it tended to be down to these main factors.

Not Doing Well On An Assignment:

This one is major for me personally and I know it is for a lot of people. Since I am a good student (or try to be), meaning I work hard, do the reading and everything else that a good student is meant to do. Including working hard on assignments, be it essays, exams or reports.

So whenever my essay grades come back, I felt so down and disappointed, and after a few essay scores… well, they just became annoying.

This was especially true during my second year

because I tried everything. I researched essay writing, I talked to other students and seminar leaders and I got my friend to give me his essay from the last project so I could see what he did. (Bear in mind he got an 85 on his essay)

I looked through it, made notes, I did everything.

I wrote an essay, really hoping to improve my essay writing (not that it could get much worse) and I got my results.

And I got a 58.

2 points away from a 60!

I was not impressed so I felt down and I wasn't satisfied in my learning whatsoever.

Now the reason why I'm being so honest with you is simple. Even people (like me) who know these topics like the back of their hands, don't always do well on essays. Therefore, this is partly a remind about everyone struggles with essays from time to time.

However, the second part is, I'm still here, enjoying university and learning.

I recovered from these blows by focusing on the future since everything I do for my degree will benefit me in the future. Since I'll be able to go on to do a Masters, maybe a PhD and then get a good job potentially.

Then I focused on the smaller details because I had improved with that score of 58 (no I won't tell you what I was originally but it was still in the 50s thank you very much). Therefore, I knew I needed to focus on the small victory of improving just a little bit.

And if I can improve once. I can do it again, and again, and again.

Overall, when you're feeling down, focus on the long term and what you have learnt from experience. Due to from my essay experience, I now know a better structure for essay writing so even though I haven't done as well as I wanted to, I still improved and I was learning.

So-called Boring Topics:

Let's face it, there will be topics we don't enjoy at university, but they're part of the syllabus so you have to learn them. Also sometimes the topic themselves won't be *boring*, it's the way the lecturer is talking about them.

However, when you come across a *boring* topic, your engagement levels will drop and you will believe that you're wasting your time. Because why should you be learning this topic when you could be doing other things?

I remember this happening to me a few times and the solutions were simple.

Firstly, I made myself power through because of the long term focus, I knew this pain and suffering would help me in the future. As if it was in an exam then I'll be able to answer questions on it, get a higher mark and improve my degree overall.

Secondly, I didn't procrastinate. I think procrastinating is probably the worse thing you could do in this situation because the longer you have this *boring* topic waiting for you to do, the less productive you'll be. As this *boring* work will be on your mind and it will suck the enjoyment out of your day until you do it. Which is why I recommend just getting it done.

Finally, notice how throughout this section I've put the word *boring* in italics. That's because nothing is actually *boring*, it's all a mindset to you and what's *boring* to you might be fascinating to someone else. I know lots of people find Statistics *boring*, but I know people who find it interesting. (And no, I have no idea why)

Overall, some others for helping you feel good and self-satisfied with your learning is focus on the long term, don't procrastinate and change your mind around boredom.

<u>Active Class:</u>

My final tip for you is to use Active Class because it can really help you to manage your time, keep on top of things and plan your time better. This is great for feeling good in your learning because it means you won't be overwhelmed as you'll be able to manage your time better.

Active Class will also allow you to see what you need to do, what topics you need to cover and what tasks you have left, allowing you to plan better and keep on top of your tasks. Meaning that Active Class allows you to eliminate three stressors that would cause you to feel down and not satisfied with your learning.

Conclusion:

To wrap up this post, I need to remind you that there will be times at university and in life in general that you feel down and not satisfied with your learning. This is normal and I hope through being so honest with you that I've helped you to accept that more.

Therefore, when you feel like this, try the following solutions:

- Focus on the long term
- Focus on the smaller details to see you've learnt something and improved.
- Don't procrastinate
- Change your Mindset around boredom
- Use Active Class

Learning isn't meant to be boring. Learning is amazing, fun and mind opening so enjoy it and embrace learning!

HOW TO DEAL WITH STRESS AND ANXIETY WHEN WAITING FOR EXAM MARKS?

If there was ever a truer post about university life and mental health it would so be this one. If you're a current psychology student then you so know what I'm talking about, whether it's a psychology exam or coursework mark you're waiting for.

Sometimes the waiting is never ever fun, but this chapter will definitely help you with those feelings and it might even be a little perspective changing.

This is a must read!

How To Deal With Stress and Anxiety When Waiting For Exam Marks?

After recently going through this myself, I understand why some students get stressed and anxious whilst they wait for their university marks. Personally, I had to wait to find out if I was going on my placement year and the uncertainty of my next university year was awful.

In this post, I'll explain some tips and tricks to help you deal with this stress and anxiety. Mainly we'll be focusing on the mental health side of this topic because this is what can harm you over time.

<u>Why Is Waiting for Exam Marks Stressful?</u>

I wanted to add this section because I really want you to know that you aren't the only university student feeling like this. We all get nervous, anxious and stressed out about our exams.

After an entire year of hard work, hard deadlines and almost impossible lectures, we need to know we've done well.

We need to know we've been successful.

Sadly, there's a large time delay between our exams and us getting our results. This can't be helped but it's still stressful.

<u>Enjoy The Time Delay</u>

My first big tip to you is reframe how you see this time delay between the exams and results. Don't see this as a scary time until you know your fate for the next university year.

See it as an amazing reward and three months off university for you to enjoy. This links to the other blogs on the website about Relaxation and enjoying yourself.

Therefore, I suggest you make the most of this time by going out with friends and family, doing what you love and having fun. Because I know from experience it isn't long until you're back at university again!

Your Feelings Are Temporary

I borrowed this tip from a podcast I'll link to down below and this is important. Due to your feelings of stress and anxiety are temporary. You aren't going to feel them forever.

As a result, you can bear this in mind, allow yourself to feel what you're feeling but know these feelings will go away.

Other Stress Reduction Tips:

I could easily talk about stress reduction for ages but we need to talk about the marks themselves. Therefore, here are two articles you might want to read:

[New Ways To Deal With Stress By Connor Whiteley](#)

[The Ultimate Stress Reducer According to A New Study By Connor Whiteley](#)

The University Marks

With this being the source of a person's anxiety and stress, it's important to talk about them.

First and foremost, there are just marks. They are your results on a standardised test that show your knowledge at a point in time. They aren't the end of the world and if you're reading a blog like this then chances are, you've tried your best. That's all anyone can ask of you.

Expectations of Marks and Getting What You need

Leading me onto another point, please don't set your expectations too high. For example one of my university friends, he's extremely smart and he rightfully sets his expectations high. But he was disappointed with a 75 before because he expected an 80 something.

At the end of the day, that result is still a very good first but he got disappointed because his expectations were off.

In terms of you, I want to say adjust your expectations accordingly to protect yourself from disappointment. For example, we know the standard is a 2:1 at university which is at least a 60. As well as with a 2:1 you can get into graduate programmes (hopefully), do years in industry and more.

Therefore, if you're stressing out that you need a first or a score of 70. Ask yourself why? Are you setting expectations higher than needed?

Of course, try to get a first (if you want) but it's okay if you only get a 60.

Conclusion:

Overall, the point of this blog post is to emphasise I know waiting for university marks is horrific. But you need to relax and focus on the free time you now have.

However, if your marks are concerning you then make sure you understand you only need to get what you need for your next stage of university.

I know this is a very difficult topic but I hope you found it useful.

If you want, please check out these two articles for more relaxation tips:

New Ways To Deal With Stress By Connor

Whiteley

The Ultimate Stress Reducer According to A New Study By Connor Whiteley

Have a great day!

WHY IS TALKING SO POWERFUL FOR UNIVERSITY STUDENTS?

To finish up the first part of this book, I wanted to finish on looking at an area of… self-development I suppose you could call it and that is to do with talking.

Now I mention presentations and other university skills in another university guide but I wanted to include this here so you can benefit, become more confident and maybe focus a little on the mental health perspective.

But the chapter is a lot more than just mental health. Enjoy!

Why Is Talking Powerful For University Students?

I have probably mentioned it before but one of the many things that I like about doing these posts is I get to learn things constantly. For example, this post should be going out in July, which turns out is the Samaritans' *Talk To Us* awareness month. Therefore, I wanted to address this issue more broadly from a mental health and wider perspective about the power of us university students actually talking to others about ourselves. There are a range of reasons why we should do this more and should look at it, so if you're interested in your mental health and a university student. This post is definitely for you!

Why Look At Talking For University Students?

Whilst the UK is a rather extraverted culture and I know that other parts of the world are no different. Yet all these cultures are very introverted when it comes to certain topics for various reasons. For example, few people talk about mental health openly because of all the cultural rubbish about "men don't show emotion" and the rest of the utter rubbish that is just head shaking.

Also very few people talk about growing confidence and using talking to help you with that. As well as you might be thinking there are tons of different resources, talks, etc. on growing confidence and public speaking. But there is a critical flaw in all of those resources. They are done by people who are extroverted, make their money with it and aren't that relatable to introverts.

As well as there are other reasons why, but talking and actually opening up at university can be very helpful. That's the focus of today's blog post.

Why Is Talking Powerful For University Students? The Mental Health Perspective:

Considering my background is psychology and mental health I would be remiss if I didn't mention it at least briefly, and this is the area that the Samaritans focus on.

However, as we know from plenty of different pieces of research, if you hold in your struggles and concerns and difficulties. Then your mental health does suffer and that damages you for the long term, and increases your risk of a breakdown or depression.

Therefore, as I've mentioned before on this blog and my own podcast, talking to others and actually telling them what's going on really can help you. It might help you to see the solutions to your problems, how to deal with what is bothering you and most importantly it doesn't make you weak in the slightest.

If you want to learn more, definitely check out my post on: How To Find Mental Health Support Services For Students?

Additionally, the reason why I'm brief in the above sections is because I've mentioned it before. Yet I haven't mentioned or focused as much on the need for us to talk to others about they are and their mental health.

As well as there are plenty of great benefits to doing that.

Firstly, it makes them realise how great of a friend you are, because you're taking the time to find out how they actually feel (instead of them just quickly saying they're fine because that's the British thing to say). Then it can lead you to open up about yourself too because you can both share your experiences and realise you aren't alone and you can both plan how to sort out your situation together. Probably deepening the bonds of your friendship even further.

Overall, actually taking the time to talk to your friends and family can have great benefits for you, them and your mental health. Therefore, definitely try to make time for this "deeper" level of conversation and talk to your friends and see how they are.

Growing Confidence:

As I mentioned on my Pride focused post topic, there are times when I literally create a title for these posts and I just write. I have no idea where I'm going and at some point subheadings pop up. This post is absolutely no exception, but talking can have great benefits to grow your confidence.

The idea of this came from a comment a family friend made yesterday when I was out with them, because they mentioned how her son working in a pub had increased his confidence.

Of course, I am not saying you should all suddenly decide to work in a bar.

However, I am saying making and encouraging yourself to talk to others might seem like baby steps but if you aren't naturally confident. Then it can be great steps towards building your confidence and if you can speak to anyone easily, then public speaking and presentations will be a lot easier too.

I know this is true from my university Outreach work as a Student Ambassador. As a result of me having to talk with students, teachers and help the lead ambassador do whatever they're doing. It forced me out of my comfort zone and it did increase my confidence, which is why I'm actually looking forward to September as I'll be doing it and seeing great people again.

Additionally, whilst this was meant to be another section, I've basically mentioned it here ready. But talking to other people, being social and more can really help you make the most of your time at university. Since university might only be three years for you, so you might as well try to make it the best three years of your life. Try to make as many connections and opportunities for yourself, make as many friends as you can and just have fun. Of course study too but you get the idea.

You truly do get out of university what you put in, and that goes for the social just as much as the academic side.

Overall, definitely start talking to other people at university. They're likely to be just as unsure about talking to others as you are, and you might make a friend, make a new connection and increase your confidence too. If you don't try talking to someone, you will never know where that conversation can take you.

And believe me, sometimes you can end up with some very surprising opportunities just because of a tiny conversation.

Conclusion:

As I mentioned earlier, I wrote this post because July is the Samaritans' *Talk To Us* awareness month, which focuses on mental health. Yet I wanted to go beyond that and focus on what are the other great benefits of talking to others, trying to push yourself and being more social. I know I have spoken about this all before and it is scattered in other posts. Yet now you have it all in a single post blog focusing on the great benefits of talking.

And I know talking to so-called random strangers can be scary, but you need to remember this critical fact. Everyone at university is there to learn, they have the same concerns and difficulties as you. Therefore, you are never alone and you never know how much of an impact on someone else's life you might have by you taking the first step and talking to them.

So talk to people, make friends and make the most of university.

For most people university might just be three years. But those three years don't have to be dull or uneventful. They can be the best three years of your life, but only if you take the first steps towards that happening.

And it all begins with talking.

PART TWO: THE UNIVERSITY MINDSET

THE UNIVERSITY MINDSET

The next part of the book is definitely something you won't find in the classroom, library or lecture theatre (but saying that if you find this book useful then definitely consider asking this to be added to your university library. It might help a lot of other students).

However, my personal problem with universities is that they just expect you to know certain things and that includes mindset.

They just expect you to have a certain mindset.

However, that isn't true because mindset is learnt to a large extent, so this next part of the book is just critical if you want to have the mindset of a successful university student.

The University Mindset

In today's post I've decided to borrow a concept from my writer self because it really does apply to university. Since to become a successful writer, all the professional writers (Nora Roberts, Dean Wesley

Smith, Stephen King and more) have certain attitudes and a certain mindset. As a university student, you need to have certain attitudes and mindsets too.

I know I won't cover all of the university mindset topic today but I'll properly be doing follow up posts at some point.

Ways To Think About The University Mindset:

In case you didn't get the writer analogy, an easier way to explain it, is when you take a step back from the successful, mid and unsuccessful university students you tend to see certain patterns emerge.

As well as now I think about it there are stages of sorts so people can easily learn these attitudes and hopefully progress to become more successful at university.

This is why the University Mindset is important to learn because it's easier for some people to have the right attitudes towards university and that can allow them to do really well. But other people come to university, have a shock because university was harder or very different from their expectations, and need to learn this mindset.

In addition, this can even happen between years or stages at university. Since with the first year of university being a step down from A-Level, IB or whatever your local equivalent, this can mean students don't need to develop this university mindset straight away. Leading to a rather extreme shock in second year when the workload piles up.

Lastly, I want to really stress that attitudes can be

learnt and sometimes you can think you have these attitudes but you don't. I'll talk about this in the future but when I got to university in 2019 I thought I had the right attitudes and everything to allow me to get the grades I wanted. This wasn't arrogance, it was just me knowing I needed to learn, study and have fun too. But compared to other students I don't have the mindset so there's room for me to improve too.

Overall, the point of this blog post is to help you realise there are some attitudes that would be helpful at university and you can learn these attitudes. Then we'll explore more of these in future posts.

What Does The University Mindset Cover?

Again I do need to refer to a writing example because it's the easiest way for me to flow the information to you so you can learn this. (Experienced writers might like my joke!) Therefore, just like how the professional author mindset can be broken down into attitudes towards writing, publishing and business. The University mindset can be broken down too.

With the areas of the university mindset being attitudes towards the Topic, Reading, Learning, Relaxation and Improvement. Reading I've decided to include as a separate field because reading is a broader topic than learning and I think involves different attitudes.

Attitudes Around Topic

I have mentioned this before in other posts but I want to hammer it home here because if you go to university please make sure you LOVE the topic you're going to be studying. This love will drive you through the tough times and it will be your driving force during your degree.

In addition, this ties into your career because your love for the topic will be your driving force but your future career could be a goal for you. Yet a career goal helps I think but it isn't a hundred precent needed.

I remember a lot of my old 6th form friends (16-18 education in the UK) who went to different universities to do psychology and other degrees. Only for them to drop out and not do their degree.

You know why?

Because they didn't care about their degrees enough. They didn't have a love and a drive when it comes to their topics.

On the other hand, I remember two other great people I went to school with, one boy, one girl and they really love their topics. The boy does business at Surrey and the girl does biology (I think) at my university. I don't see them but we have mutual friends and I know they're loving their degrees because they have a love for the topic.

Of course, I know their degrees (like all of them) will be hard but they love the topic so much they don't want to do anything else, and that drive makes them successful students.

As well as I'm the same, it's my drive and love for psychology that makes me keep going when the times get tough and I really, really don't want to do my degree anymore. It's the learning that keeps me going. Sure, I think essay writing is pointless because no one does it in the real world but I still do it because it allows me to learn.

<u>Conclusion:</u>

In our quick introduction post to the University Mindset, we've covered a lot of the basics and I've got you thinking about the topic of your degree and how much you love it. Will it be enough to sustain you in the tough times?

Whatever the answer, I wish you the best of luck with your university journey.

THE LEARNING UNIVERSITY MINDSET

Again this is another introduction where the intro to the actual post is far better than I can resummarise here. Yet for psychology students (and this is more aimed at newer ones), you will learn amazing things about human behaviour, the mind and why we do what we do.

Yet you cannot learn any of this without having a mindset that wants to learn, and that's where this post comes in.

<u>The Learning University Mindset</u>

Continuing our look at the University Mindset, we need to look at one of the most important (and obvious) aspects of the University Mindset- learning. Since if you have a bad mindset around learning at University then you could struggle and it might harm your chances of thriving at university.

I know some people reading this might be thinking this is odd to talk about because surely if you're going to go to university then you would have to love learning.

If you thought that I can't blame you, but even at university I've seen too many people see learning as this boring, evil thing that is a chore and not enjoyable. Resulting in some of these people leaving university and not going on to their future ambitions.

Thankfully your mindset around learning can be changed.

How To see Learning At University?

Personally I see learning as an amazing thing because learning can give you great knowledge that others don't have, learning can give you access to higher paying jobs and learning can sometimes be a gateway to new passions.

But what makes learning truly great in my opinion?

It gives you a chance to study what you love and that's how I see learning at university. Learning isn't some evil chore or something that nerds do.

Instead learning is about exploring your passions and collecting knowledge so hopefully you can use it in the future to better yourself.

Of course, this sounds like I'm talking about jobs and future careers. To some extent I am because the knowledge you get in your degree can help you get into new careers and explore new paths. Which was one reason why I chose psychology because you can't get a job in psychology without a degree.

However, education and learning can also benefit

you in other ways. For example, the reason why I love forensic psychology is because it benefits you in everyday life and it helps you to overcome some of the collective biases that people have. Such as my favourite piece of knowledge I've got from that module was the media bias, how the media focuses on the most sensational stories because that's what gets people to react.

I love that fact because I can use it in everyday life so I know when a story is just a story and being exaggerated. It's really helped me in my life to sort through the news sources to find trusted ones.

My point is learning isn't bad. It's fun, exciting and it can benefit you in ways you've never expected.

But how do you see learning as fun?

<u>Do What You Love:</u>

I know this has been a repeated theme throughout my blog posts but that's because it's critical.

If you don't choose a degree subject that you love and want to study then you will start to see learning as a chore. No one likes chores. Meaning you'll stop wanting to learn, avoid it and that will be reflected in your marks.

I don't want that for you. I want you to be successful at university and your mindset is a big part of this.

Therefore, pick something you know you're going to enjoy over the years and you want to study and learn about. As I said in the first Mindset post, it's this drive and love for a subject that will help you through the tough times.

<u>Break Tradition:</u>

I needed to add in a fun subtitle here because when it comes to learning, sometimes you need to break tradition. Since at university the traditional ways of learning are reading and lectures.

Of course, still go to these critical things.

But also add in some types of learning that break tradition massively. For example, I don't recommend this unless you want to but I write books as part of my learning. I write books using what I've learnt then I write it so it's fun, engaging and interesting. That's another part of my learning.

Some more normal ways to learn include study groups and talking with friends. If you're friends with people in your cohort then talk to them about learning and what you're studying. Practice explaining it to each other like they don't know what it means or talk about it with your parents.

Chances are your parents are like mine. They don't have a clue about psychology so I can tell them and teach them too.

All of this can be great fun and actually quite funny but it's all still learning.

And that's what's important about the Learning Mindset, it isn't necessarily about how hard you study or learn or how dedicated you are. It's about your willingness to learn, how much you enjoy it and you're proactive about your education.

Because if you love your subject, you keep learning and you keep expanding what you know. Then from my own experience and those of friends, this will almost certainly be shown in your work and your marks will reflect that.

<u>Conclusion:</u>

After reading this, I hope you now have a better understanding of learning at university because I know lots of people say it's hard, it's evil and boring as hell.

It isn't.

It's all about how you look at it and how you approach it.

I approach all sorts of learning, be it writing, psychology or business, with fun and excitement because every so often I discover a massive life changing piece of information that I love.

And I can honestly say it's these moments that make it all worth it for me.

So please keep learning, have fun and you never know what you might find.

WHAT IS THE IMPROVEMENT UNIVERSITY MINDSET?

Another way to put this chapter is basically how do you improve at university. You'll see why I felt the need to do this chapter later on, but universities are rather bad, in my opinion, at explaining how to improve at university.

But there are ways to do so.

So if you want to improve at university and get higher grades then this is a perfect place to start!

<u>What Is The Improvement Mindset At University?</u>

On our penultimate mindset post, we're going to be talking about improvement at university and for me, this is a very important post because I think this is my weakest mindset area because this is something I actively need to improve on. So you aren't alone and hopefully we can improve in this area together.

<u>Why Is Improvement Important?</u>

Like everything, you need to improve at university and there will always be ways to improve.

Believe me, university markers (rightfully) love to point out all the small and big ways how you can improve. From improving the structure of your essay to writing the discussions in your reports, there are always ways to get better.

Furthermore, improvements become more and more important each academic year because your first year at university is easy compared to the second and third. As well as it's only your second and third year that count towards your final degree classification. This is great because it means you can find out how you do at different assessments in your first year and know how to improve for your second and third.

Overall, if you want to do well at university, I would unofficially recommend you keep wanting to improve, write better essays and always strive to do better.

Of course the flip side, I don't want you to get stressed out about improving so always try and find a balance between relaxing, learning and improving. This will become clearer in the rest of the blog post.

How Can You Improve At University?

One of my flaws at university is that I don't do enough of these options below because university in general is great for students who want to get better. Since, at least at my university, there are lots of resources and opportunities for you to read things online or speak to people in person about how to improve your work.

Therefore, I'm telling you this for two reasons.

The first is if you feel like you should be doing more to improve, you aren't the only one. But both of us need to take a leap and be proactive about how to improve because it will benefit our degrees. The second is I want you to know you aren't alone at university. There are ways for the university to help you if you're struggling with assessments.

Use What's Available:

Now this very much depends on the university itself but I cannot imagine any university doesn't have this type of support.

Anyway, my university has a Student Learning Advisory Service which offers two kinds of support: online and in-person. The online support includes lots of great articles and online documents about how to write better, how to research, organise your writing and more. This is great because it provides generalised support that's available immediately. Thus, you can read it and find out how to improve.

I've done this before and I do recommend everyone try it. I know I've found it helpful before but on some topics, I feel like it's a bit too general. As well as the advice for how to improve depends on the degree and the school too.

For example, I study psychology so I need to write scientifically in the American Psychological Association 7th Edition manner. Which is completely different to how a law student or media studies student would write.

In this case, definitely check out your school and

what's available for you specifically.

Again, I know there are things available from my school, like emailing my academic supervisor, but sometimes I don't feel confident enough to go and talk to them. Also it doesn't help that I'm terrible for explaining myself properly. But this isn't an excuse for me or you not to go out and seek these opportunities for help because I'm doing this blog post to make myself ask for help more so I can improve.

In fact, I'll be doing that a lot this year for my placement projects.

All in all, I know it can seem scary or too much effort to get help from your university. Yet we both need to think about it like this, the successful university students go out of their way and actively want to improve. They enjoy improving and want to get better so they can get better grades for their degree.

That's how we need to think about it. Improving is needed but it can be a fun learning experience like I mentioned in the last Mindset post.

Read Academic Papers:

I know this sounds horrific to a lot of students but I promise you it works and I realised this last week. Due to at the moment, I'm on my placement year and I went through my First and Second year of university without reading an academic paper outside of what was needed. Even then I only tended to read the abstract and conclusion, you'll be amazed what you can learn from those two sections alone!

However, for my placement I need to write an academic literature review, I've done them before, but I really wanted to focus on this one since it was for my placement. Therefore, I read this great literature review done by my Placement Supervisor and his PhD student and I made notes and I thought nothing more of it. I left it for the weekend but when it got to Monday, and I started to write the literature review. I was very surprised to know that my academic writing seemed to improve a lot and I understood how to write a lot more.

Consequently, I know it doesn't sound exciting but I promise you reading academic papers is a great way to improve your academic writing skills. As well as if you read ones on topics you enjoy then this can be fun.

So try it and have fun!

Use The Internet:

Finally, there is nothing stopping you from doing your own research to improve. Reading academic papers and looking at what your university offers are both great options that I highly recommend. But sometimes you need someone else to tell you things so you can fully understand it.

You could look at YouTube Videos about academic writing.

You could read articles from other universities or students about essay writing.

All these can be helpful to you, so be proactive and have a look around. You never know what you might find.

There have been plenty of times when I've found YouTube videos to be helpful to me and online articles, so try it for yourself.

<u>Conclusion:</u>

Overall, this area of mindset isn't spoken about and it is avoided by most students. This doesn't make you a bad student and this is something we all need to work on. I know I need to work on this area as well as I know this post has been useful to me so I can think about how I can improve in my academic writing.

Therefore, I know this wasn't the most exciting mindset area, but it's still critical.

So please, research how to improve, use your university, use academic papers, use whatever helps you. But remember to keep learning and having fun too.

However you decide to improve and help your university mindset, I wish you all the best of luck with your university journey!

THE UNIVERSITY MINDSET AND READING

To finish off the content of this book before the conclusion, we need to talk about reading. Not only because it is a critical piece of university life but because there are a lot of myths, misconceptions and negativity we need to address.

And as psychology students, believe me, you will have a lot of reading at different points in your university life.

So this is probably one of the most important chapters in the book!

<u>The University Mindset and Reading:</u>

To conclude this mini-series about the university mindset, we need to look at reading. Because let's face it, at university you'll be set chapters and papers to read each week depending on your course and you need to do them. The lecturer doesn't set these for fun, I actually doubt they want to flick through textbook after textbook or paper after paper trying to find students things to read. I think they would prefer to do the other million tasks they have to do.

Anyway, the whole point of these readings are to help further develop your learning because there's only so much that can be taught in a two hour lecture. As well as these readings are to help you learn about becoming an independent learner and understanding the vocabulary of academia.

However, when students come to university, they tend to think these readings don't matter, they're pointless and it's the lecturer trying to waste their time.

Of course this isn't a good mindset to have around reading because this sort of negative mindset ties into other areas. And I truly believe that your attitudes towards reading tie into your beliefs about learning. Meaning if you hate reading then you'll probably hate learning too and as we've seen in other posts, a hate of learning can be damaging at university.

Where Do Negative Attitudes Towards Reading Come From?

As always this is just my own opinion, yet these attitudes tend to come from two places. One- it comes from the student not wanting to learn and be actively involved in their learning. Two- it comes from the student buying into the myths about how easy university is and you don't need to do half the things you're set.

The Reality:

Now let's unpack both of those areas.

When it comes to a person wanting to learn and improve their knowledge as part of their degree, as I mentioned before, you need to be proactive about it. You need to explore beyond what you're set in classes and we all do this in different ways. Personally, I read extra book chapters from time to time on topics I'm interested in. For example, I recently read a great chapter of a book on Police Psychology.

Therefore, students need to change their thinking about reading as part of learning and that it's fun.

Will all chapters and readings be interesting?

God no. I have read some truly boring papers in my time but it was all part of learning and I made sure I tried at least. I made sure I approached the reading as something interesting and fun, not some evil chore that was going to ruin my life.

Since I've learnt some of my favourite psychological facts outside of the lecture theatre and inside readings. For example, the "What The Heck Effect" and various thinking biases.

Therefore, I know I've said this before in different contexts but I truly do believe reading is great and it can be fun. It won't always be but there will be times when you read something interesting and it will shock you. The "What The Heck Effect" did that for me.

So what will you discover in your readings?

Believing The Myth of Ease at University:

Now this myth is based in some truth because the first year of university doesn't count towards your final degree classification and it's a step down from your 16-18 year old education (Whatever it's called in your country).

However, this myth becomes deadly if students waste an entire year and don't develop the critical skills needed for the second and final year of your degree. I spoke more about this in the learning mindset post because if you start to learn the tricks of the successful Student Mindset early, then it becomes easier later on.

I know I found it easier than a lot of people in my cohort.

All in all, my advice here is from a mindset perspective, definitely use your first time to have fun and make new friends. I cannot stress that enough. But also use it as a time to develop new skills and see if you need to change your mindset around certain topics.

And again this isn't some evil mind-changing chore, look at it as changing your perspective so you can do better in your degree for your future.

Mini-Series' Conclusion:

As we come to the end of this mini-series, I hope you've now started to understand the power of a mindset around university. As well as how it can help you do better in your degree so you can benefit for years to come.

In addition, the main theme of this series has been one simple thing: have fun or at least enjoy the process. In the grand scheme of things, you don't spend a lot of time at university so have fun with it, learn as much as you can, make friends and try not to see anything as a chore. If you have a university mindset centred around learning is fun, interesting and beneficial then the passion and interest will show in your work. Hopefully leading to better marks. But if it doesn't, you've still had fun anyway.

Also I should mention again that I am not perfect in my university mindset, I love learning and I am passionate about psychology. But I'm far from a perfect university student. As well as I'm saying this to encourage you that this mindset is a marathon and not a sprint. And that at the end of the day, I'm just like you.

So whatever you decide to do with this mindset information, I hope you enjoy your time at university and I wish you the best of luck on your university journey. Wherever it may take you!

CONCLUSION

I want to start wrapping up this book by mentioning something I talk about a lot on The Psychology World Podcast, talking about mental health and protecting it doesn't make you weak, pathetic, non-manly or any of the other utter rubbish society tries to teach us about mental health.

Mental health is very, very real.

And I really hope that after this book you've started to get a firmer understanding of how to protect yourself from the negatives of bad mental health, where you need to go if you need help and the sorts of mindsets that are very useful at university.

Personally I actually would have loved to have this sort of book available to me as a brand-new student. Due to I would have loved to know how to protect my mental health, how to overcome imposter syndrome and the other mindsets that would be useful to me at university.

I really do wish that universities, lecturers and

student unions as a whole did more to actually talk to students about improving at university and adopting new mindsets to help them. Instead of just assuming that everyone who comes to university always has what they need.

No.

However, that was one of the reasons why I wrote this book in the first place. I wanted to bring all these blog posts together in a certain order that would take you wonderful reader through a journey that is similar to the university journey.

And I truly hoped that it helped.

<u>Next Steps:</u>

In these university guides, I really want to help you even more by offering a few suggested next steps that might help you further on your university journey, so I have three for you.

Firstly, I would definitely implement what is relevant from these posts into your own life. For example, see what mental health support services your current or future university offers (you never ever know when it might be useful not only to you but friends as well).

Secondly, check out the other university guides in the series wherever you bought this book from. All of them are filled with useful information about different parts of the university journey that might really help you.

And like this book, they're all really engaging, intriguing and have a personal conversational tone

(You can see how much I hate boring dull textbooks, can't you?).

Finally, you definitely might want to check out my psychology books in *An Introductory Series* and listen to *The Psychology World Podcast*. Because I am always surprised and extremely grateful for the readers who email, tweet me or comment saying how much they enjoy the books and the podcast and how much they learn.

And lots of students and even psychology professionals have found the different books useful in their university journey, and we do cover almost every single area of psychology at this stage either in books or on the podcast.

So definitely check them out!

Overall, I really hope you enjoyed the book and please remember to look after your mental health at university, and having the University Mindset. You'll be surprised at how just looking after yourself can really benefit the rest of your life (both social and academic).

https://www.subscribepage.com/psychologyboxset

Thank you for reading.
I hoped you enjoyed it.
If you want a FREE book and keep up to date about new books and project. Then please sign up for my newsletter at
www.connorwhiteley.net/
Have a great day.

CHECK OUT THE PSYCHOLOGY WORLD PODCAST FOR MORE PSYCHOLOGY INFORMATION! AVAILABLE ON ALL MAJOR PODCAST APPS.

About the author:

Connor Whiteley is the author of over 60 books in the sci-fi fantasy, nonfiction psychology and books for writer's genre and he is a Human Branding Speaker and Consultant.

He is a passionate warhammer 40,000 reader, psychology student and author.

Who narrates his own audiobooks and he hosts The Psychology World Podcast.

All whilst studying Psychology at the University of Kent, England.

Also, he was a former Explorer Scout where he gave a speech to the Maltese President in August 2018 and he attended Prince Charles' 70th Birthday Party at Buckingham Palace in May 2018.

Plus, he is a self-confessed coffee lover!

All books in 'An Introductory Series':
BIOLOGICAL PSYCHOLOGY 3RD EDITION
COGNITIVE PSYCHOLOGY THIRD EDITION
SOCIAL PSYCHOLOGY- 3RD EDITION
ABNORMAL PSYCHOLOGY 3RD EDITION
PSYCHOLOGY OF RELATIONSHIPS- 3RD EDITION
DEVELOPMENTAL PSYCHOLOGY 3RD EDITION
HEALTH PSYCHOLOGY
RESEARCH IN PSYCHOLOGY
A GUIDE TO MENTAL HEALTH AND TREATMENT AROUND THE WORLD- A GLOBAL LOOK AT DEPRESSION
FORENSIC PSYCHOLOGY
THE FORENSIC PSYCHOLOGY OF THEFT, BURGLARY AND OTHER CRIMES AGAINST PROPERTY
CRIMINAL PROFILING: A FORENSIC PSYCHOLOGY GUIDE TO FBI PROFILING AND GEOGRAPHICAL AND STATISTICAL PROFILING.
CLINICAL PSYCHOLOGY
FORMULATION IN PSYCHOTHERAPY

PERSONALITY PSYCHOLOGY AND INDIVIDUAL DIFFERENCES
CLINICAL PSYCHOLOGY REFLECTIONS VOLUME 1
CLINICAL PSYCHOLOGY REFLECTIONS VOLUME 2
CULT PSYCHOLOGY
Police Psychology

A Psychology Student's Guide To University
How Does University Work?
A Student's Guide To University And Learning
University Mental Health and Mindset

Companion guides:
BIOLOGICAL PSYCHOLOGY 2ND EDITION WORKBOOK
COGNITIVE PSYCHOLOGY 2ND EDITION WORKBOOK
SOCIOCULTURAL PSYCHOLOGY 2ND EDITION WORKBOOK
ABNORMAL PSYCHOLOGY 2ND EDITION WORKBOOK
PSYCHOLOGY OF HUMAN RELATIONSHIPS 2ND EDITION WORKBOOK

CONNOR WHITELEY

<u>HEALTH PSYCHOLOGY WORKBOOK</u>
<u>FORENSIC PSYCHOLOGY WORKBOOK</u>

OTHER SHORT STORIES BY CONNOR WHITELEY

<u>Mystery Short Stories:</u>
Poison In The Candy Cane
Christmas Innocence
You Better Watch Out
Christmas Theft
Trouble In Christmas
Smell of The Lake
Problem In A Car
Theft, Past and Team
Embezzler In The Room
A Strange Way To Go
A Horrible Way To Go
Ann Awful Way To Go
An Old Way To Go
A Fishy Way To Go
A Pointy Way To Go
A High Way To Go
A Fiery Way To Go
A Glassy Way To Go
A Chocolatey Way To Go
Kendra Detective Mystery Collection Volume 1
Kendra Detective Mystery Collection Volume 2
Stealing A Chance At Freedom

Glassblowing and Death
Theft of Independence
Cookie Thief
Marble Thief
Book Thief
Art Thief
Mated At The Morgue
The Big Five Whoopee Moments
Stealing An Election
Mystery Short Story Collection Volume 1
Mystery Short Story Collection Volume 2

Science Fiction Short Stories:
The First Rememberer
Life of A Rememberer
System of Wonder
Lifesaver
Remarkable Way She Died
The Interrogation of Annabella Stormic
Blade of The Emperor
Arbiter's Truth
Computation of Battle
Old One's Wrath
Puppets and Masters
Ship of Plague
Interrogation
Edge of Failure

One Way Choice
Acceptable Losses
Balance of Power
Good Idea At The Time
Escape Plan
Escape In The Hesitation
Inspiration In Need
Singing Warriors
Knowledge is Power
Killer of Polluters
Climate of Death
The Family Mailing Affair
Defining Criminality
The Martian Affair
A Cheating Affair
The Little Café Affair
Mountain of Death
Prisoner's Fight
Claws of Death
Bitter Air
Honey Hunt
Blade On A Train

<u>Fantasy Short Stories:</u>
City of Snow
City of Light
City of Vengeance
Dragons, Goats and Kingdom
Smog The Pathetic Dragon
Don't Go In The Shed
The Tomato Saver
The Remarkable Way She Died
The Bloodied Rose
Asmodia's Wrath
Heart of A Killer
Emissary of Blood
Dragon Coins
Dragon Tea
Dragon Rider
Sacrifice of the Soul
Heart of The Flesheater
Heart of The Regent
Heart of The Standing
Feline of The Lost
Heart of The Story
City of Fire
Awaiting Death

Other books by Connor Whiteley:

Bettie English Private Eye Series
A Very Private Woman
The Russian Case
A Very Urgent Matter
A Case Most Personal
Trains, Scots and Private Eyes
The Federation Protects

The Fireheart Fantasy Series
Heart of Fire
Heart of Lies
Heart of Prophecy
Heart of Bones
Heart of Fate

City of Assassins (Urban Fantasy)
City of Death
City of Marytrs
City of Pleasure
City of Power

Agents of The Emperor
Return of The Ancient Ones
Vigilance
Angels of Fire
Kingmaker

The Garro Series- Fantasy/Sci-fi
GARRO: GALAXY'S END
GARRO: RISE OF THE ORDER
GARRO: END TIMES
GARRO: SHORT STORIES
GARRO: COLLECTION
GARRO: HERESY
GARRO: FAITHLESS
GARRO: DESTROYER OF WORLDS
GARRO: COLLECTIONS BOOK 4-6
GARRO: MISTRESS OF BLOOD
GARRO: BEACON OF HOPE
GARRO: END OF DAYS

Winter Series- Fantasy Trilogy Books
WINTER'S COMING
WINTER'S HUNT
WINTER'S REVENGE
WINTER'S DISSENSION

Miscellaneous:
RETURN
FREEDOM
SALVATION
Reflection of Mount Flame
The Masked One
The Great Deer

Audiobooks by Connor Whiteley:
BIOLOGICAL PSYCHOLOGY
COGNITIVE PSYCHOLOGY
SOCIOCULTURAL PSYCHOLOGY
ABNORMAL PSYCHOLOGY
PSYCHOLOGY OF HUMAN RELATIONSHIPS
HEALTH PSYCHOLOGY
DEVELOPMENTAL PSYCHOLOGY
RESEARCH IN PSYCHOLOGY
FORENSIC PSYCHOLOGY
GARRO: GALAXY'S END
GARRO: RISE OF THE ORDER
GARRO: SHORT STORIES
GARRO: END TIMES
GARRO: COLLECTION
GARRO: HERESY
GARRO: FAITHLESS
GARRO: DESTROYER OF WORLDS
GARRO: COLLECTION BOOKS 4-6
GARRO: COLLECTION BOOKS 1-6

Business books:
TIME MANAGEMENT: A GUIDE FOR STUDENTS AND WORKERS
LEADERSHIP: WHAT MAKES A GOOD LEADER? A GUIDE FOR STUDENTS

AND WORKERS.
BUSINESS SKILLS: HOW TO SURVIVE THE BUSINESS WORLD? A GUIDE FOR STUDENTS, EMPLOYEES AND EMPLOYERS.
BUSINESS COLLECTION

GET YOUR FREE BOOK AT:
WWW.CONNORWHITELEY.NET

www.ingramcontent.com/pod-product-compliance
Lightning Source LLC
LaVergne TN
LVHW011848060526
838200LV00054B/4234